"MAKE YOUR ACTIONS REFLECT YOUR WORDS."

— Severn Cullis-Suzuki

Groundwood Books / House of Anansi Press
groundwoodbooks.com

We gratefully acknowledge the Government of Canada for their financial support of our publishing program.

Canada Council   Conseil des Arts
for the Arts   du Canada

ONTARIO ARTS COUNCIL
CONSEIL DES ARTS DE L'ONTARIO
an Ontario government agency
un organisme du gouvernement de l'Ontario

With the participation of the Government of Canada   Canadä
Avec la participation du gouvernement du Canada

Library and Archives Canada Cataloguing in Publication
Title: Severn speaks out / speech by Severn Cullis-Suzuki ; commentary by Alex Nogués ; illustrated by Ana Suárez ; translated by Susan Ouriou.
Other titles: Hagan que sus acciones reflejen sus palabras. English
Names: Nogués Otero, Alex, author. | Container of (work): Cullis-Suzuki, Severn. Severn speaks out. | Suárez, Ana, illustrator. | Ouriou, Susan, translator.
Description: Series statement: Speak out series | Translation of: Hagan que sus acciones reflejen sus palabras. | Speech originally presented in 1992 in English. Text of speech translated into Spanish, Catalan, and Portuguese and published in 2019. Analysis of speech by Alex Nogués originally published in Spanish, Catalan, and Portuguese, and translated from the Spanish into English for this edition.
Identifiers: Canadiana (print) 20210395982 | Canadiana (ebook) 20210396008 | ISBN 9781773068879 (hardcover) | ISBN 9781773068886 (EPUB)
Subjects: LCSH: Cullis-Suzuki, Severn. Severn speaks out—Juvenile literature. | LCSH: Environmental protection—Juvenile literature. | LCSH: Conservation of natural resources—Juvenile literature. | LCSH: Ecology—Juvenile literature. | LCSH: Cullis-Suzuki, Severn—Juvenile literature. | LCSH: Environmentalists—Canada—Juvenile literature. | LCGFT: Speeches.
Classification: LCC TD170.15 .N6413 2022 | DDC j363.7—dc23

The illustrations were created with mixed media.
Design by Inês Castel-Branco and Danielle Arbour
Printed and bound in South Korea

SEVERN
SPEAKS OUT

Speech by Severn Cullis-Suzuki | Commentary by Alex Nogués
Translation by Susan Ouriou | Illustrations by Ana Suárez

GROUNDWOOD BOOKS   HOUSE OF ANANSI PRESS   TORONTO / BERKELEY

Contents

SPEECH

KEYS TO THE SPEECH

SPEECH DELIVERED BY SEVERN CULLIS-SUZUKI AT THE EARTH SUMMIT

Rio de Janeiro, June 11, 1992

Hello, I'm Severn Suzuki,

speaking for ECO, the Environmental Children's Organization. We are a group of twelve- and thirteen-year-olds trying to make a difference: Vanessa Suttie, Morgan Geisler, Michelle Quigg and me.

We've raised all the money to come here ourselves, to come 5,000 miles to tell you adults you must change your ways.

Coming up here today, I have no hidden agenda. I am fighting for my future.

Losing my future is not like losing an election or a few points on the stock market.

I am here to speak for all generations to come.

I am here to speak on behalf of the starving children around the world whose cries go unheard.

I am here to speak for the countless animals dying across this planet, because they have nowhere left to go.

"I am here to
speak for all
generations
to come."

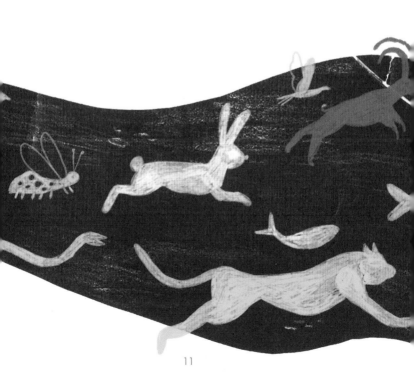

I am afraid to go out in the sun now because of the holes in our ozone.

I am afraid to breathe the air because I don't know what chemicals are in it.

I used to go fishing in Vancouver, my home, with my dad, until just a few years ago we found the fish full of cancers.

And now we hear of animals and plants going extinct every day, vanishing forever.

In my life, I have dreamt of seeing the great herds of wild animals, jungles and rainforests full of birds and butterflies, but now I wonder if they will even exist for my children to see.

"...but now I wonder if they will even exist for my children to see."

Did you have to worry of these things when you were my age?

All this is happening before our eyes and yet we act as if we have all the time we want and all the solutions.

I'm only a child and I don't have all the solutions, but I want you to realize, neither do you! You don't know how to fix the holes in our ozone layer. You don't know how to bring the salmon back up a dead stream. You don't know how to bring back an animal, now extinct, and you can't bring back the forests that once grew where there is now a desert.

If you don't know how to fix it, please stop breaking it!

"If you don't know how to fix it, please stop breaking it!"

"In my anger, I am not blind, and in my fear, I am not afraid of telling the world how I feel."

Here, you may be delegates of your governments, business people, organizers, reporters or politicians — but really you are mothers and fathers, sisters and brothers, aunts and uncles — and all of you are someone's child.

I'm only a child yet I know we are all part of a family, 5 billion strong; in fact, 30 million species strong, and borders and governments will never change that.

I'm only a child yet I know we are all in this together and should act as one single world towards one single goal.

In my anger, I am not blind, and in my fear, I am not afraid of telling the world how I feel.

In my country, we make so much waste; we buy and throw away, buy and throw away, buy and throw away, and yet northern countries will not share with the needy. Even when we have more than enough, we are afraid to share, we are afraid to let go of some of our wealth.

In Canada, we live the privileged life, with plenty of food, water and shelter. We have watches, bicycles, computers and television sets. The list could go on for two days.

"...we are afraid to share, we are afraid to let go of some of our wealth."

"If a child on the streets, who has nothing, is willing to share, why are we, who have everything, still so greedy?"

Two days ago here in Brazil, we were shocked when we spent time with some children living on the streets. This is what one child told us: "I wish I was rich and if I were, I would give all the street children food, clothes, medicines, shelter, and love and affection."

If a child on the streets, who has nothing, is willing to share, why are we, who have everything, still so greedy?

I can't stop thinking that these are children my own age; that it makes a tremendous difference where you are born; that I could be one of those children living in the favelas of Rio; I could be a child starving in Somalia, or a victim of war in the Middle East, or a beggar in India.

I am only a child yet I know if all the money spent on war was spent on finding environmental answers, ending poverty and finding treaties, what a wonderful place this earth would be!

At school, even in kindergarten, you teach us how to behave in the world. You teach us to not fight with others, to work things out, to respect others, to clean up our mess, not to hurt other creatures, to share and not be greedy.

Then why do you go out and do the things you tell us not to do?

Do not forget why you're attending these conferences, who you're doing this for. We are your own children. You are deciding what kind of world we are growing up in. Parents should be able to comfort their children by saying "everything's going to be all right," "it's not the end of the world" and "we're doing the best we can."

"We are your own children. You are deciding what kind of world we are growing up in."

But I don't think you can say that to us anymore. Are we even on your list of priorities?

My dad always says, "You are what you do, not what you say."

Well, what you do makes me cry at night.

You grown-ups say you love us. But I challenge you, please make your actions reflect your words.

Thank you.

"I challenge you,
please make your
actions reflect
your words."

KEYS TO THE SPEECH

A child steps up to the podium. The world falls silent listening to her.

Commentary by Alex Nogués

Translated by Susan Ouriou

Hello, world. I am Severn Suzuki.

From June 3 to 14, 1992, the world officially opened its eyes... or that's what it felt like. Every country on the planet was invited to the Earth Summit organized by the United Nations in Rio de Janeiro, Brazil. The goal: to agree together on a global roadmap and commitments to make any development a nation undertakes conditional on the needs of natural ecosystems; to slow down the indiscriminate logging of forests; to protect the planet's biodiversity; and to reverse — or at least slow — global warming, already identified and increasingly understood. Basically, for the first time, an attempt was being made to ensure that human progress would be supportive of the planet's health. The concept of *sustainable development* was adopted, one that we had never before managed to fully grasp or believe in. In 1992, there was clearly concern already over the devastating toll progress was taking on Nature. In 1992, we had begun to catch a glimpse of the monster we had unleashed, and it was coming for us.

In this context, on June 11, on behalf of a children's organization, a twelve-year-old girl was about to walk up to the podium to address the delegates and stand up and be heard.

Her name was Severn Cullis-Suzuki.

As I write these lines, that child is now thirty-nine years old and devotes her life to protecting the language, customs and natural territories of the Haida in British Columbia, Canada, where she lives with her husband and two children. When she was only fifteen, she was ceremonially adopted into the Wolf Raven clan of Tanu of the Haida Nation by Chief Chee Xial, Miles Richardson Sr. They gave her the name Kihlgula Gaay.ya, which means "Good Speaker."

Good speaker indeed.

There is no doubt there.

Let us go back to June 11, 1992.

A child steps up to the podium.

The world falls silent listening to her.

"Hello, I'm Severn Suzuki."

I have come to fight. I have come to wake you up.

Soon they will learn that she has traveled 5000 miles (8000 km) with her friends — companions fighting and hoping by her side. She has come to tell the truth, to confront the world's leaders with it. She does not hide: "Hello, I'm Severn Suzuki." Hers is an act meant to educate, yes, but above all it is an act of courage. It is not only a speech, it is a warning. I am a child, I have come to fight, and I am not afraid of you.

Her voice rings with conviction and a sense of urgency at what needs to be done: awakening consciences at a crucial time. She makes it clear from the start that she is there to demand answers and, especially, action from the adults of the world, and to insist that they change their ways. She speaks to the world's rulers not only in their capacities as leaders, politicians or strategists, but also as sisters and brothers, fathers and mothers.

What of Severn's parents? Who are they? She comes by her activist spirit and her gift for communication naturally. Her father is David Suzuki, a renowned scientist and famous television broadcaster, and her mother is Tara Cullis, a writer, environmental activist and cofounder of ten organizations, including the David Suzuki Foundation.

"I am fighting for my future," Severn says.

She looks up.

Pauses.

"I am here to speak for all generations to come."

She looks up.

Pauses.

Severn is afraid her own children will never see the jungles or rainforests full of birds and butterflies. She feels that fear in the here and now. When you're a child, time does not exist. When you are an adolescent, time is infinite. Once you have children, time is an urgency for their future and all futures.

On June 11, 1992, Severn became an intergenerational advocate, someone to defend coming generations that day and every day since. Fighting for the present and all the presents to come. Still, is there such a thing as an intergenerational crime? Think of the forest. Cutting down a forest that took centuries to grow means depriving many other generations of its existence. Denying them the air it purifies, the water it holds in place, the shade, the scenery, the hiking, the berries, the firewood it provides. To deprive them of the forest is to deny them spring and autumn, games among the trees, fallen branches for forts.

We should be asking our children, grandchildren, great-grandchildren and great-great-grandchildren whether the reasons for logging that forest are warranted. However, until someone invents a time machine that would allow for such a utopian democracy bridging centuries, any decision to decimate a forest should not be taken without first weighing, for instance, the consequences its disappearance would have three hundred years down the road.

And what of soil? Soil is the foundation of everything, of forests, of farming, and it plays a crucial role in filtering and cleaning the water that reaches aquifers and rivers. It takes little time to remove it. In one hour, a single backhoe is capable of eliminating dozens of cubic yards of soil. How long before it builds up again? In this case, we could be looking at thousands of years. Depriving dozens of generations, and thousands and thousands of species of plants and animals of soil without a highly defensible reason founded on the common good could be seen as a crime against humanity. Forests and soil should be among our most revered assets, and yet they are among the most undervalued. Soil lost to human activity is disappearing at a rate of 100 billion tons per year.

Just a child speaking about other children?

Representatives from 172 participating countries had spent nearly ten days grappling with data as devastating as that presented above, and with long and difficult negotiations. To make matters worse, they seemed to be making little headway. The United States was strongly opposed to the principles and treaties being discussed at the summit and, indeed, refused to sign the Convention on Biological Diversity.

The delegates were exhausted, as evidenced by a few clips from the video filmed during the speech, but they look up to listen to the voice of this girl who is able to explain the situation so plainly and with such conviction.

Severn is only a child, as she says, but she has come to speak clearly and forcefully of the cries of starving children that no one listens to.

At the Rio Summit, as at so many others, the world's greatest contradictions are in evidence. In Rio de Janeiro, the array of security, hotels, charter flights and banquet spreads must have been quite impressive. Presidents and ministers are not accustomed to living within modest means.

Severn and her companions had just come from speaking to the children of the favelas where people are crammed together with no running water, plumbing or medicine, with only enough food to avoid dying of hunger and with not even the shadow of a future. Perhaps world leaders do not see or do not wish to see the stark contrast between the two realities, but the child Severn, in her innocence, cannot help but notice that the privileged life she leads in Canada could not be further removed from that of the children of Brazil's favelas. How can we be so stingy? We have nothing for them and so much for ourselves . . .

Children are children wherever they may be. They have hopes. Dreams. They have rights! One of which is to live in a healthy environment.

The salmon, our salmon, are full of cancers.

Severn tells her audience she used to go angling in the river with her father, until one day they found fish full of cancers. A nightmare? No. A harsh reality.

Antonio Sandoval, an environmental educator, bird lover and brilliant writer, coined the word *naturalgia* to describe the despair one feels at the destruction and degradation of Nature.

A crushing feeling that no one should ever have to experience.

Nature is us. It is not just our home, a beautiful landscape or a source of resources and recreation. We are Nature. We exist thanks to (and as part of) a long and enduring chain of delicate balances struck to overcome thousands of hazardous events.

"Everything depends on everything else," say the Haida. And they are so right.

This is something they already knew while the colonizers had forgotten.

Today animals and plants are becoming extinct at an unheard-of rate.

We are here to talk about this! Severn exclaims.

Naturalgia brought her here, far from home. She and her friends have taken the reins, ready to confront a giant.

Greed

What lies at the heart of the problem is the economy. Why are we so greedy? Severn asks.

In the market economy, individual people with first and last names and their own particular microeconomies matter less than macroeconomic parameters. The stock market's ups and downs. Annual growth. Risk premiums. Gross domestic product. That is what counts. According to Merriam-Webster's dictionary, gross domestic product (GDP) is "the gross national product excluding the value of net income earned abroad." Does GDP really measure what matters? Can the stock market tell us how happy people are?

Value as seen by the stock market should not serve as our guide. Severn speaks of Values with a capital V: peace, respect, doing no harm to other creatures, cleaning up our messes, sharing . . . Everything adults teach small children but then refuse to uphold themselves. Why such senselessness? What kind of irrational duplicity is this? Severn cries.

In a forceful tone, she reminds every delegate of the why of their presence, and for whom they do what they do. The decisions they make will shape the world in which their children will grow up.

Everything's going to be all right?

Severn wonders whether the fathers and mothers of the world can continue to be able to comfort their children by saying things like, "everything's going to be all right," "it's not the end of the world" or "we're doing the best we can." Can those who were children in 1992 still say the same thirty years on? And you, reading these pages, if you are young today, can you demand that your parents be accountable? If you are a grown-up, can you answer in all good conscience?

Tough questions.

The great writer Kurt Vonnegut, when invited to speak at a commencement ceremony, said, "Whenever my children complain about the planet to me, I say, 'Shut up! I just got here myself! Who do you think I am — Methuselah?'"

In 2010 in the documentary *Severn: la voix de nos enfants [Severn: The Voice of Our Children]*, Severn Cullis-Suzuki, expecting her first child at the time and reflecting on the eighteen years that had followed her famous speech, could not help but become emotional. We see a grown-up Severn who has learned that the war is never over and that the enemy is powerful and uncaring. There have been occasional victories but many battles have been lost over the years. We cannot say we are better off now — rather, just the opposite.

The inertia inherent in human affairs is mind-boggling. Time marches swiftly on, yet change takes place slowly, often swinging one way then back. Young people should always be there to rouse us from our mindless lethargy. The time you have in which to accept and fulfill that responsibility is nothing but the blink of an eye.

Persuasion as a weapon of mass transformation

Together we must fight, using Severn's words as our banner, without reproach and with conviction.

A fight for human beings, for justice, for beauty.

Act, learn, change, protect, speak out, convince, persuade. Follow Severn's lead.

Young Severn's speech is perfect and has much to teach us. It is the essence of persuasion. She uses the first person, relentlessly engaging the audience with rhetorical questions, pauses and a focused gaze. Her tone is serious and varies depending on the arguments she raises, sometimes troubled, at others indignant. However, make no mistake: "In my anger, I am not blind, and in my fear, I am not afraid of telling the world how I feel." Not only is she not blind, but with each sentence, each assessment, she shows great lucidity. Not only is she not afraid to tell the world how she feels, she does so by making use of all the elements any good speech should include, as the Greeks already knew twenty-four centuries ago:

Ethos (credibility): Something very difficult for a child of twelve to show, but that problem is soon resolved: We have travelled more than 5000 miles, we raised the money to come here. We are an environmental organization. Furthermore, with her serious, determined demeanor, she quickly erases any doubt. She speaks of what she knows. As the child she is, she speaks of the children she visited in the favelas where they live. She speaks of what is taught in kindergarten and school.

Pathos (emotion): Severn speaks of going fishing, her father, her dreams, her fears. She shows herself to be both vulnerable and caring. She describes her experience in the favelas. She reminds those gathered that they are each part of a family, some with children of their own, but all someone else's child, and she calls for them to engage in the fight she has come to champion.

Logos (active reasoning): Here Severn has no need to provide further data, graphs or predictions. The delegates have just spent days listening to scientists expose the harsh reality, backed by a plethora of details and reports. The context itself is one of sheer *logos*.

Her speech is replete with the figures of speech used in rhetoric, in particular repetition and accumulation. "I'm only a child," she repeats, and "I am here to speak." She underscores the main ideas using mechanisms that help to reinforce one clear and powerful message: do right by your children, and if you don't know how to fix the world, then stop breaking it!

One day she will be Kihlgula Gaay.ya.

May our actions reflect our words

Watching the video of her speech, you will note changes in the audience's expressions and attitude. One delegate from Belize looks into the camera then lowers his gaze, ashamed. I live in Spain, so I looked for Spain's representatives. Just as Severn says, ironically, "we're doing the best we can," a representative from Japan appears onscreen and, behind him, the nameplate for "Spain" shows in front of three empty seats. I found no reference to the speech in Spain's mainstream media of the time. In fact, the whole summit only rated at most three-quarters of a page each day in the major newspapers. Any attention paid to environmental issues in the media has not improved significantly in Spain since then. I challenge you to see for yourself in your country. Add up the number of pages in the written press or the number of minutes on television or radio covering sports and the number covering the environment. Keep it up for a couple of weeks, then draw your own conclusions.

The Spain of June 1992 was caught up in pre-Olympic pomp and ceremony and in Seville's Universal Exposition. On June 6, 1992, the newspaper *La Vanguardia* featured half a page on the Rio Summit under the following headline: "Spain outlines its plans for adapting to climate change." The other half was devoted to an advertisement for air conditioners. The brand in question boasted its "climate domination." Was the layout intentional? It must just have been a coincidence.

It will be hard to counter the destructive inertia

inherent in human affairs. Which is why you, a mother, father, daughter or son, must roll up your sleeves and get to work.

"You are what you do, not what you say," Severn concludes, paraphrasing her father. Her speech is an emotional dance somewhere between a plea and a challenge. Where is the coherence in adult behavior? Coherence is what could save us.

May your actions reflect your words.

May your actions not make children cry at night.

This does not seem like an impossible feat. We need to start now, without fail, insisting again and again on what we believe in.

Listening, deliberately, to the echoes

But to change the world, the first thing we must change is us. And for that to happen, we need to listen, deliberately.

Let us listen to the voice of Severn's mother, Tara Cullis.

She, too, was adopted by the Haida. They gave her the name Jaad Gaa Skuudagaas, which means "Woman of Knowledge." Her great struggle is to bring balance back to Western thought, which has been the cause of so much destruction. In the Western world, we overstate the importance of the left side of the brain, the reductionist and linear side, she explains. We need to bring the right side of the brain back into the thinking equation. In other words, we must promote, listen to and integrate into our economy and society Indigenous voices and those of women, poets, musicians and philosophers.

"There are constantly," says Tara Cullis, "forces trying to destroy and break us apart; I choose to be part of the forces that bring us together."

Let us also listen to the Haida: "The world is as sharp as the edge of a knife. One must take care not to fall off of it."

Reflect on your actions and consider what you do to ensure the desired consequences. The world's balance is easily upset, and it can be so very dangerous and difficult to set to rights once it has been overturned . . .

Guided by her concerns, Severn Cullis-Suzuki studied biology, specializing in ethnoecology. Ethnoecology is the science of ecology combined with the knowledge held by different human groups about traditional uses for plants and other natural resources in their environment.

Indigenous Peoples in North America have always lived in balance with the ecosystems that welcomed them. In fact, it would be more accurate to state that they have been part of that balance. They have acquired deep knowledge of the ecology of their land and how to protect its resources. We must listen and learn from them. As Severn says, inspired by their example, we must rediscover how to live in a way that will ensure our long-term survival.

Over the years, Severn herself has shifted her focus from the global fight begun almost thirty years ago to local battles on Haida Gwaii. Focus your energy on protecting the forests that still exist near your home. Demand that the stream that passes through your town flow plentiful and clear. Fight side by side with your loved ones for the ground you walk on. Convert your garden, your patio, your balcony into a flowering of hope. Think globally, act locally.

Just as Tara Cullis recommended, let us listen to the poets. American poet and environmentalist Gary Snyder summed it up in the final stanza of his poem "For the Children":

> stay together
> learn the flowers
> go light

"There was not a sound of the song of a bird. It was eerie, terrifying. What was man doing to our perfect and beautiful world?" wrote Rachel Carson in 1962 in her book *Silent Spring*, which opened our eyes to the disaster brought about then (and still today) by pesticides and intensive farming.

In 1972, Spanish naturalist and broadcaster Félix Rodríguez de la Fuente predicted on television that one day we would find ourselves drowning in plastic. He considered that "ours could very easily be called the 'Garbage Civilization.'"

In September 2013, at the United Nations General Assembly, José Mújica, the president of Uruguay at the time, mused:

We promise a life of spending and squandering, basically starting the countdown against nature and the future of humankind. A civilization opposed to simplicity, sobriety, all natural cycles, but worse still: a civilization opposed to freedom, meaning the time we need to experience human relationships.

In 2021, a member of the Old Massett Village Council on Haida Gwaii, where Severn now lives with her family, spoke about the island's ancient forests. Kuuyang-Lisa White said:

> "Our people and our lands and waters are connected. The province is burning down, the water's drying up, and we're still clear cutting old-growth forests ... What's really needed is reciprocity. It's time to give back. The people and the land need to heal."

The clamor of beauty

All the voices above and all the others we don't have room for here, perhaps heard but not heeded, must be both listened to and assimilated—knowing now that time is running out. Ecosystems have a limit, a point of no return. In our oblivion and arrogance, we do not even know if we have already exceeded that limit. If humankind's greed is such in the face of abundance, what will it be in times of scarcity?

From Nature's perspective, there is no drama. In a battle waged between humans and the wild, the latter will win. Life will have its way no matter what the adversity. We are not facing the end of life. We face the dangerous end of what we know and what we have adapted to over the past tens of thousands of years. In the unknown, humans have little chance of survival. Although this may not necessarily be the end of humankind either, we do have a sense that we are facing the end of something.

"The Garden of Eden is no more," proclaimed the great naturalist David Attenborough in 2019. We cannot continue to stand by as people die of starvation or drown in the sea. We cannot remain with arms crossed before the disappearance of yet another species, the logging of yet another primary forest, the desertification of yet another sea.

"It is the mystery which enchants, and its being extinguished with the extinction of the necessary combination of its elements." writes Friedrich Schiller, another poet. The erasure of the yet-to-be-discovered mystery of thousands of species. The transformation of a forest's meandering into a field of monoculture. The annihilation of the futures of thousands of children, their lives strangled by the greed of a few. We are face to face with the possibility of beauty's end.

Our world is made of humus and flowers, the shade of a tree, the unrestrained chirping of swallows come spring. It is the cool, transparent water of the river and the thousand blues of the sea. Our world begins in a child's embrace, a friend's smile, a loved one's kiss. Asphalt, money, engines and technology have been conceived by humans to make life more convenient, yet they dehumanize us at the same time.

We must listen and we must understand.

Renewal of hope

History repeats itself almost thirty years later. Greta Thunberg, not quite a child, not quite an adult, driven by profound naturalgia, stages a sit-in outside the parliament of Sweden, her country, at first for a full three weeks and then every Friday. It is a protest against her government's inaction in the face of the greatest disaster for which, unfortunately, humans are responsible: climate change. Her activism has given rise to Fridays for Future — a movement of young people from around the world fighting for their future.

On December 28, 2018, in Katowice, Poland, during the United Nation's twenty-fifth conference on climate change, Greta Thunberg addressed world leaders in a speech very similar to Severn's. The principal new element is the following:

> You have ignored us in the past and you will ignore us again. We have run out of excuses and we are running out of time. We have come here to tell you that change is coming whether you like it or not. The real power belongs to the people.

The real power belongs to the people.

Young people of the world, be ever mindful of the fact that you will always just have gotten here.

Adults of the world, let us not allow shame to cause us to look away.

Let us do everything we have in our power.

"You grown-ups say you love us. But I challenge you,

please make your actions reflect your words," Severn states at the end of her 1992 speech.

"You said you loved us!" proclaimed Severn in 2010. "And I'm still saying the same things now. I'm an adult, but I'm saying the same thing. Because I still believe it."

She stifles a sob.

"So, I still have a lot of hope," she says, overcoming her sorrow.

And you, reading this, are part of that renewal of hope.

Source Notes

Page 38: "Everything depends on everything else." Severn Cullis-Suzuki. Personal interview.

Page 40: "Whenever my children complain about the planet ..." Kurt Vonnegut, "How to Make Money and Find Love!" delivered at Fredonia College, Fredonia, New York, 20 May 1978. *If This Isn't Nice, What Is?* New York: Seven Stories Press, 2014.

Page 45: "There are constantly forces trying to destroy us ..." Tara Cullis quoted in "Turning Points" by Rosemary Anderson, *Trek*, 2016, pp. 8–11.

Page 45: "The world is as sharp as the edge of a knife ..." Severn Cullis-Suzuki. Personal interview.

Page 46: "stay together / learn the flowers / go light" from "For the Children" by Gary Snyder. *Literature and Medicine*, vol. 15, no. 1, Spring 1996, p. vi. Project Muse. Online.

Page 46: "There was not a sound of the song of a bird ..." Rachel Carson. *Silent Spring*. Boston: Houghton Mifflin, 1962.

Page 46: "Ours could very easily be called the 'Garbage Civilization.'" Félix Rodríguez de la Fuente, *El Planeta Azul*, "El Okavango." Aired Aug. 19, 1972 on RTVE. Online. Translated from Spanish.

Pages 46–47: "We promise a life of spending and squandering ..." *José Mujica:Soy del Sur, vengo del Sur. Esquina del Atlántico y el Plata*, delivered at the United Nations General Assembly, Sept. 2013. Translated from Spanish.

Page 47: "Our people and our lands..." Kuuyang-Lisa White quoted in "Letter from Haida Gwaii, As History Is Made" by Serena Renner, *The Tyee*, 19 Aug. 2021.

Page 48: "The Garden of Eden is no more." David Attenborough quoted in "David Attenborough tells Davos: 'The Garden of Eden is no more'" by Graeme Wearden, *Guardian*, 21 Jan. 2019.

Page 48: "It is the mystery which enchants ..." Friedrich Schiller. "Letter 1." *Letters on the Aesthetic Education of Man*. Project Gutenberg. Online.

Page 49: "You have ignored us in the past and you will ignore us again ..." Greta Thunberg, "Transcript: Greta Thunberg's Speech at the U.N. Climate Action Summit," delivered in New York, 23 Sept. 2019. NPR. Online.

Groundwood Books is grateful for the opportunity to share stories and make books on the Traditional Territory of many Nations, including the Anishinabeg, the Wendat and the Haudenosaunee. It is also the Treaty Lands of the Mississaugas of the Credit. In partnership with Indigenous writers, illustrators, editors and translators, we commit to publishing stories that reflect the experiences of Indigenous Peoples. For more about our work and values, visit us at groundwoodbooks.com.